Cinco de Mayo
Celebrating Hispanic Pride

Carol Gnojewski

Enslow Publishers, Inc.

40 Industrial Road   PO Box 38
Box 398   Aldershot
Berkeley Heights, NJ 07922 Hants GU12 6BP
USA   UK

http://www.enslow.com

To my family, friends, and Spanish language teachers.

Library of Congress Cataloging-In-Publication Data

Gnojewski, Carol.
  Cinco de mayo : celebrating Hispanic pride / Carol Gnojewski.
    p. cm. — (Finding out about holidays)
  Summary: Introduces the history, customs, and practices of this holiday commemorating the victory of the Mexican
army over the French on May 5, 1862.
  ISBN 0-7660-1575-0
  1. Cinco de Mayo (Mexican holiday)—History—Juvenile literature. 2. Mexico—Social life and customs—Juvenile
literature. 3. Mexican Americans—Social life and customs—Juvenile literature. 4. Cinco de Mayo, Battle of, 1862—
Juvenile literature. [1. Cinco de Mayo (Mexican holiday) 2. Mexico—Social life and customs. 3. Holidays.] I. Title:
5 de mayo. II. Title. III. Series.
  F1210 .G55 2002
  394.26972—dc21   2001004780

Printed in the United States of America

10 9 8 7 6 5 4 3

To Our Readers: We have done our best to make sure that all Internet addresses in this book were active and
appropriate when we went to press. However, the author and publisher have no control over and assume no liability
for the material available on those Internet sites or on other Web sites they may link to. Any comments or
suggestions can be sent by e-mail to comments@enslow.com or to the address on the back cover.

Photo Credits: ©1995 All Rights Reserved. Cartesia Software, p. 22; © by James Martin, May 10, 2001
(www.sanfrancisco.about.com) licensed to About.com, Inc. Used by permission of About.com, which can be found
on the Web at www.about.com. All rights reserved., pp. 26, 28, 34; © Corel Corporation, pp. 14, 20, 27 (bottom), 29
(top), 30, 36 (top); 44, 45, 46, 47; Dover Publications, Inc., p. 21; Enslow Publishers, Inc., p. 39; Geoff Apold,
TxDOT, p. 40; Hemera Technologies, Inc., pp. i, ii, iii, 9, 11 (both), 12, 15, 18, 23, 24 (both), 25 (top), 29 (bottom),
31, 32 (both), 33, 36 (bottom) 37 (both); Jack Lewis, TxDOT, pp. 7, 17, 38; J. A. Wrotniak, p. 8; J. Griffis Smith,
TxDOT, p. 41; Kevin Stillman/TxDOT, pp. 5, 27 (top), 35; Library of Congress, pp. 6, 10, 13, 16, 19; 25 (bottom);
Texas State Library and Archives Commission, p. 4.

Cover Photos: © by James Martin, May 10, 2001 (www.sanfrancisco.about.com) licensed to About.com, Inc.
Used by permission of About.com, which can be found on the Web at www.about.com. All rights reserved.
(background, middle inset); Kevin Stillman, TxDOT (top inset); Library of Congress (bottom inset).

CONTENTS

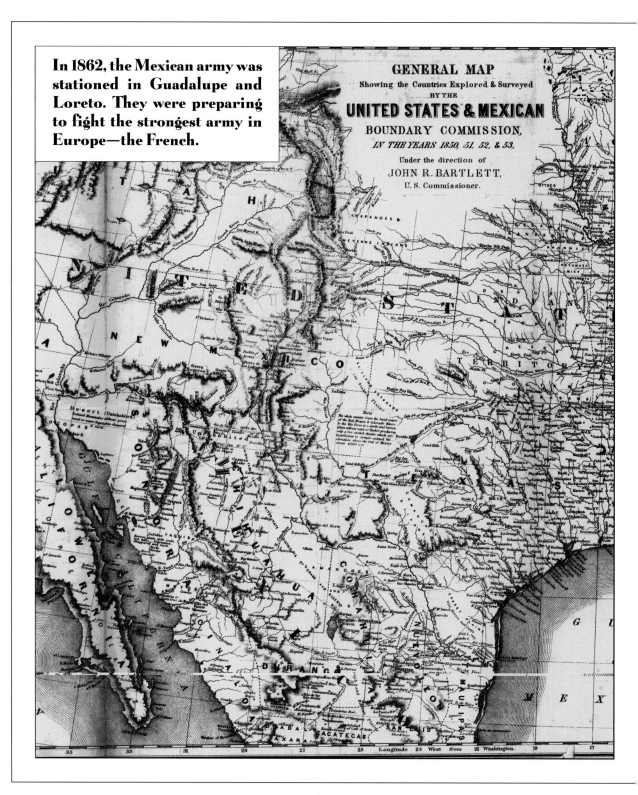

In 1862, the Mexican army was stationed in Guadalupe and Loreto. They were preparing to fight the strongest army in Europe—the French.

CHAPTER 1

Benito Juárez

On May 5, 1862, the Mexican army waited in its forts. It was on top of the tall hills of Guadalupe and Loreto. The army was made up of an inexperienced but tough group of men. Many soldiers had never fought before. Few had guns or uniforms. And they were going to fight against the strongest army in Europe.

Everyone knew that the French army was coming. It was marching to Mexico City, the capital city of Mexico. It wanted to take over the new Mexican government. The

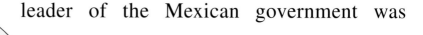

leader of the Mexican government was President Benito Juárez. Cinco de Mayo celebrates the victory of the Mexicans over the French in this important battle.

Benito Juárez was a Zapotec Indian. Some people call him the Mexican Abraham Lincoln. Like President Lincoln, he grew up poor. He was born in 1806 in a small country village. His parents were native Mexicans. They died before he was three. Benito and his sisters grew up without parents. They were orphans. Their grandparents and uncles raised them.

Young Benito worked all day in the fields. There was no school in the village. So, one of Benito's uncles taught him how to read. Benito wanted to get a better education. When he was thirteen, he left home. He moved to the nearby

Benito Juárez was a great Mexican leader.

city of Oaxaca (wha HA kah). His older sister worked there as a cook. In Oaxaca, a kind bookbinder adopted him. The bookbinder sent Benito to school.

At school, Benito noticed that the rich children had better teachers than the poorer children and the Indians did. He did not think this was fair. Benito had to study extra hard to learn to read and write well. He became interested in the history of his country. He wanted to know why life was easier for some people than for others.

Young Benito worked hard in the fields all day.

Chichén Itzá was a famous city built by ancient Mayas.

CHAPTER 2

Mexico Gains Its Freedom

Mexico is home to many different groups of people. Native people lived there for thousands of years. Mayas, Toltecs, Zapotecs, and Aztecs are some of these groups. The ancient people built large and beautiful cities. They made stone pyramids that pointed toward the sun.

Spanish soldiers called conquistadores (con KEYS ta doors) came to Mexico from Europe in 1521. They were looking for gold that they thought was in Mexico. They took over the land and the people living there.

Mexico now belonged to Spain. Mexicans were forced to work for the conquistadores. The

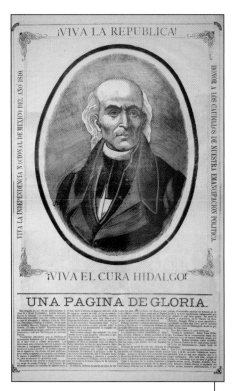

¡VIVA LA REPUBLICA!

¡VIVA EL CURA HIDALGO!

UNA PAGINA DE GLORIA.

This is a drawing of Father Miguel Hidalgo. The Spanish words in this picture read, "Long live the Republic! Long live Father Hidalgo! A page of glory."

Mexicans were not treated well. Father Miguel Hidalgo became the leader of the Mexican people. He taught the Mexicans about democracy.

In a democracy, all people have the right to decide how they want to live. On September 16, 1810, Father Hidalgo started a revolution. He told the Mexicans to fight for their freedom. Their fight lasted more than ten years.

By 1821, the Mexican people had gained their freedom from the Spanish. The people of Mexico began to make their own rules and laws. It was a very hard thing to do. They were not used to being in charge and figuring out their own future.

Different groups within Mexico could not agree. Each wanted to take control. These groups began to fight each other. At the same time, Mexico borrowed money from other countries to grow stronger.

Then, the United States started a war against Mexico. The Mexican-American War lasted from 1846 to 1848. It divided the people in Mexico even more. Mexico lost the war. The United States won land that had belonged to Mexico. This land became the states of Arizona, California, Colorado, Nevada, New Mexico, and Utah.

Meanwhile, Benito Juárez found a way to make things better in Mexico. He was a lawyer and a governor. He stopped those in power from taking land away from native Mexicans. He worked to pass laws that made everyone in the country equal. After the Mexican-American War, the Mexican people were tired of fighting. They needed an honest

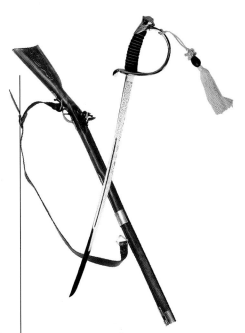

The United States became friends with Mexico after the Mexican-American War.

11

and brave leader like Benito Juárez to bring them together.

WHAT LED TO CINCO DE MAYO?

Benito Juárez became the president of Mexico in 1860. But Mexico was a weak country. It owed money to many other countries. England, Spain, and France wanted to be paid the money they were owed by Mexico. Benito Juárez had a hard choice to make. Should he pay back what his country owed or use the money to make Mexico stronger? He decided to help his people. He asked the countries he owed money not to ask for it back for two years.

England, Spain, and France were not happy. They thought that Mexico had a lot of gold and silver and should be able to

England, Spain, and France wanted the Mexican people to pay what was owed to them in gold and silver pieces.

pay back what it owed. They sent soldiers to get the money, but the English and Spanish soon left Mexico. The French did not.

Louis Napoleon was the ruler of France. He knew that Mexico was fighting to stay alive. He also knew that the United States could not help Mexico if France invaded. After the Mexican-American War, Mexico and the United States were *amigos*. This means that they were friends. But the United States was busy fighting the Civil War on its own land. Louis Napoleon planned to take over Mexico. If the French could do this, they might also be able to stop the United States from growing bigger and stronger. Napoleon's army took over the port city of Veracruz. Then, it began the long march to Mexico City.

Louis Napoleon was the ruler of France in the 1860s.

The Mexicans fought to be freed of French rule.

CHAPTER 3

The Battle of Puebla

On the afternoon of May 5, 1862, the French army was getting close to the city of Puebla. President Juárez gave the order to fight. General Ignacio Zaragoza and the Mexican army got ready to fight the French.

Ignacio Zaragoza was a Mexican general from the American state of Texas. The Mexican people did not want the French in their country. They came from nearby villages to help General Zaragoza and his army push the French out. They wanted to keep their homes and families safe.

Farmers, shopkeepers, and ranchers brought

GUERRE DU MEXIQUE . SIÈGE ET PRISE DE PUÉBLA.   Imp.Lith.Ch.Pinot éditeur

The Mexican people rose up together to battle the French.

long knives and farm tools to use as weapons. Mexican cowboys arrived on horseback. They carried spears and curved swords. Zapotec Indians gathered sticks and stones to throw. They carried large signs with drawings of Mary, the mother of Jesus. They prayed to her. They asked her for the strength to win the coming battle.

It did not bother General Zaragoza that the French had many more soldiers than the Mexicans did. He knew the land and his soldiers well. When the French general asked him to give up, he was ready. But he did not wait to see what the French would do. Instead, he sent one of his generals and some troops on horseback to surprise the French forces. The

French troops could not catch the Mexicans. Some French soldiers were captured. Others got lost or were separated from their troops.

General Zaragoza ordered the Mexican troops to gather as many bulls and cows as they could find. They let the angry animals run straight toward the French troops. Then, it

The French troops were caught in a stampede of cattle that the Mexican army had directed toward them.

The French army's cannons became stuck in the mud, and the rain ruined their gunpowder.

began to rain. Some French soldiers slid in the mud. Their carts and cannons got stuck in the deep holes. Hail started to fall. The wet weather ruined the powder needed to fire guns and cannons.

The French charged up the hills three times. Each time they had to turn back. After four hours of fighting, they gave up. They marched back to their base. Mexican teamwork had saved the day. By working together, the army and the townspeople won the Battle of Puebla.

That battle was won. But the war was not over. The Mexican people could not celebrate for long. A year later, the French army came back to Mexico. Some 30,000 French soldiers came back and took over the forts at Puebla. Then they marched on and took over Mexico City. Benito Juárez left the capital. He was replaced by a man named Maximilian Hapsburg. Some wealthy Mexicans wanted Hapsburg to be the ruler of Mexico. They were landowners and businesspeople. They hoped Hapsburg would help them protect their money.

Wealthy Mexicans wanted Maximilian Hapsburg to rule Mexico.

But Hapsburg and the wealthy Mexicans did not think alike. Hapsburg wanted to keep the new laws that made life fairer for all Mexicans. Like Juárez, he believed in education. He was not interested in helping the wealthy landowners and businesspeople get richer.

But the Mexican people had not

Even though the Mexicans had won the Battle of Puebla, the French returned a year later and took over Mexico City.

forgotten the lesson of the Battle of Puebla. They knew that they could be powerful if they worked together. They knew they could fight and win. They had to beat the French again.

Benito Juárez led the Mexicans against the French for three long years. He had even received help from Abraham Lincoln. Lincoln ordered American troops to supply Juárez with weapons.

On June 5, 1867, Juárez came back to Mexico City. He took over running the country. Finally, the French left Mexico. And Benito Juárez was Mexico's president again.

Abraham Lincoln had the United States supply the Mexican troops with weapons so that they could defeat the French army.

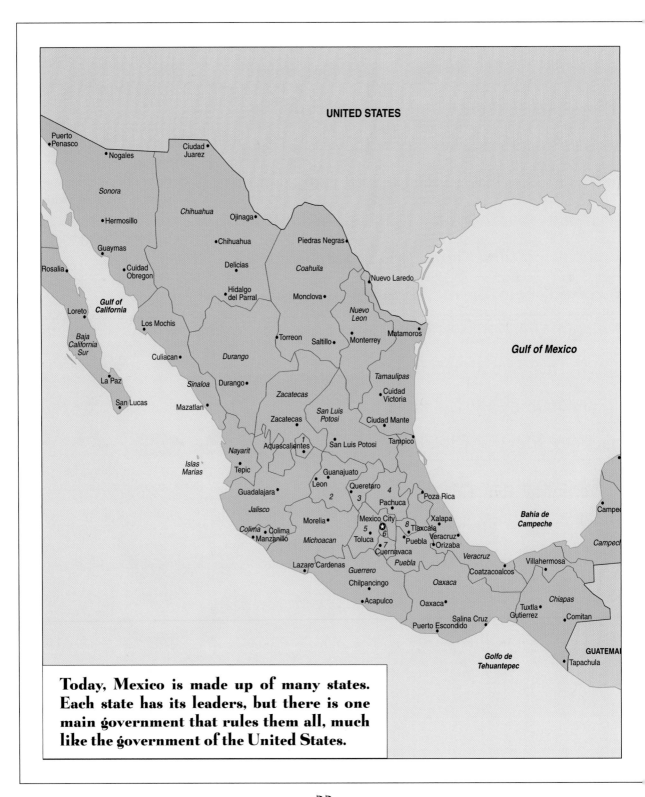

UNITED STATES

Puerto
Penasco
Nogales
Ciudad
Juarez

Sonora

Chihuahua
Ojinaga
Hermosillo

Guaymas
Chihuahua
Piedras Negras

Rosalia
Cuidad
Obregon
Delicias
Coahuila

Nuevo Laredo

Hidalgo
del Parral
Monclova

*Gulf of
California*
Loreto
Los Mochis

*Nuevo
Leon*
Matamoros

Torreon
Saltillo
Monterrey

*Baja
California
Sur*

Culiacan
Durango

La Paz
Sinaloa
Durango
Tamaulipas

San Lucas
Mazatlan
Cuidad
Victoria

Zacatecas

Zacatecas
*San Luis
Potosi*
Ciudad Mante

Nayarit
Aguascalientes
1
San Luis Potosi
Tampico

*Islas
Marias*
Tepic
Guanajuato

Guadalajara
Leon
Queretaro
4
Poza Rica

*Bahia de
Campeche*

Jalisco
2
3
Pachuca

Campec

Morelia
Mexico City
Xalapa

Colima Colima
5
8 Tlaxcala
Veracruz

Campech

Manzanillo
Michoacan
Toluca
6
Puebla Orizaba

7
Cuernavaca
Veracruz

Lazaro Cardenas
Puebla
Coatzacoalcos
Villahermosa

Guerrero
Chilpancingo

Oaxaca

Chiapas

Acapulco
Oaxaca
Tuxtla
Gutierrez
Comitan

Salina Cruz

Puerto Escondido

*Golfo de
Tehuantepec*

GUATEMAL
Tapachula

Gulf of Mexico

**Today, Mexico is made up of many states.
Each state has its leaders, but there is one
main government that rules them all, much
like the government of the United States.**

CHAPTER 4

Mexico Today

MEXICAN FOLK SONGS

★

Mexican folk songs are called corridos. There are many famous songs that are in Spanish, but one of the best-known corridos is "La Cucaracha," a song about a cockroach that cannot walk.

With help from Benito Juárez, Mexico got stronger. Juárez was a great leader. He helped to make changes in the laws. The government was run differently. Today, Mexico is made up of many states or regions. But there is one main government that rules over them all. It is very much like the kind of government that we have in the United States. Each state has its own leaders. But the country is ruled by a president.

Mexico has thirty-one states. Mexico City is the capital of the country. Rules for everyone are made there. Each

Pesos are spent in Mexico instead of dollars.

The Mexican flag is made up of stripes of red, white, and green.

state has its own state capital, too. Most Mexicans speak Spanish. They buy food and clothes with pesos and centavos instead of dollars and cents. The colors of the Mexican flag are red, white, and green.

Puebla is the capital city of the state of Puebla. It is an hour-and-a-half drive from Mexico City. Puebla sits at the bottom of two volcanoes. The city's official name is Puebla de Zaragoza. After the battle it was named for General Ignacio Zaragoza. The name honors the Mexican general who led the troops during the Battle of Puebla.

If you travel to Puebla, you will find old stone homes. There are also buildings with large archways, patios, and balconies. People can walk through paved streets and town squares. These are some of the same places where French soldiers had marched more than one hundred years before.

People can also visit the ruined forts of Guadalupe and Loreto. One fort is a war museum now. It has a display of hundreds of toy soldiers. The soldiers show how the French and Mexican soldiers fought during the Battle of Puebla. The battlefield is now a park. In the park there is a statue of General Zaragoza.

Beautiful hand-made pottery has always been sold in the streets in Puebla.

These drummers want to sound their best on Cinco de Mayo

CHAPTER 5

Remembering Those Who Fought

All the brave Mexicans who fought against the French are remembered every year on Cinco de Mayo. In the Spanish language, *Cinco de Mayo* means "fifth of May." The fifth of May is celebrated all over Mexico. But it is most important in the state of Puebla and in Mexico City. These were the places that the French tried to take over.

The holiday is also celebrated all over the United States. Some towns have parades. They honor the people who would not give up until their country was free. Mexican-American groups might wear uniforms and

People walk through the streets selling flowers during Cinco de Mayo fiestas.

carry Mexican flags. School bands march and play music. They practice for months to sound their best in the parade. Families try to find the best spot to watch and listen to the parade.

In Mexico, some *barrios*, or neighborhoods, pretend to fight the Battle of Puebla again. Groups of people dress up like the French army. They wear bright blue and red clothes. Other people dress like the Mexican army or the Indians. When the pretend battle ends, the Mexicans are the winners. There is a moment of silence. Then everyone shouts, "*Viva Mexico*!" That means, "Long live Mexico!"

After the parades and battles, there is also a *fiesta* (fee ES ta) in the town square. A fiesta is a party. There are people selling food, flowers, and crafts. There are also games and carnival rides. Musicians walk through the streets. They play lively music. Dancers in costumes do traditional dances. Everybody has fun. They eat, sing, and dance.

Children in costume watch the parades and dancing on Cinco de Mayo.

On Cinco de May, people like to sing and play traditional Mexican songs.

CHAPTER 6

Mexican Music

Music is an important part of Cinco de Mayo and other Mexican fiestas. Mexican folk musicians are called mariachis (mar ee AH cheese). Mariachi is a Coca Indian word. It means "musician." A mariachi group is like a walking orchestra. Guitars, violins, harps, and trumpets are some of the instruments that mariachis use.

Two unusual instruments they play are the guitarrón (ghee tar OWN) and the vihuela (vee WELL ah). A guitarrón looks like a big guitar with a large belly. It has six strings that make low tones. The vihuela makes high tones. It

MARACAS

★

Maracas are rattles that are usually made from gourds, a kind of fruit that dries into a hard shell. Used as percussion instruments, maracas are often played in pairs during traditional Mexican songs.

A guitarrón (above) is a six-stringed guitar played by mariachis. The vihuela (below) is another type of guitar used by mariachis.

looks like a small, five-stringed guitar. These instruments are not used in any other kind of musical group.

Most mariachi bands have six to eight people in them. Members must know how to sing well and read music. Together, they make up songs as they walk through the crowds. Mariachis must memorize many old and new folk songs. Mexican folk songs are called *corridos* (core EE those). Corridos are songs that tell stories. Some are about famous battles and other events from history. Some talk about everyday life. Others are very funny.

When they perform, mariachis wear special clothes. They dress like *charros*, (Mexican cowboys). On their heads, they wear wide-brimmed hats called *sombreros*. Boots, short jackets, big ties, and broad belts are also part of their costumes. There are shiny metal buttons down the sides of their dark pants. Dressing up and playing music are just a couple of fun ways to celebrate Cinco de Mayo.

Mariachis dress like Mexican cowboys. They wear short jackets, big ties, and broad belts.

Traditional dances are a source of pride on Cinco de Mayo.

Mexican Dances

★

Some schools hold tardeadas, or afternoon dances, on Cinco de Mayo. All the students join in the festivities by singing, dancing, and cheering.

Dancing is another fun way to celebrate Cinco de Mayo. It is also a way for Mexican people to show pride in who they are. Traditional Mexican dances are fast and exciting. This type of dancing is called *folklórico*. Like corridos, some of these tell stories. One ancient dance is from the Huasteca region of Mexico. It is a circle dance. Dancers turn in circles. As they spin, they form circles inside of circles.

The *jarabe tapatio* (ha RA bay ta pa TEE yo) is the national dance of Mexico. It is also called

the Mexican hat dance. Men throw their sombreros to the floor. They dance around them in quick, hopping steps. Then, they stomp very hard on the floor with their heels. They are inviting the women to dance with them. Like most folkloric dances, it is a partner dance. Pairs of dancers face each other. They look into each other's eyes. Hands clap and fingers snap. Feet stomp. The music gets louder and faster. The dancers sway toward each other.

Many folklore dances are done with a partner.

Each region in Mexico has different dances. There are different costumes, or *trajes* (TRA hays), for each dance. The dancers' costumes help tell where the dance comes from. For example, the region of Jalisco (ha LEES koh)

is known for its beautiful flowers. Female Jalisco dancers look like flowers. They wear full, ruffled skirts. As they dance, they gather one edge of their skirt in their hands. Slowly, they swish it back and forth. When they twirl around, ribbons and ruffles swirl all around them. Jalisco is also known for its cowboys. The men dress in cowboy costumes like the ones that mariachis wear.

Mexican dancers wear different costumes for different types of dances.

Some dancers wear colorful scarves around their waists. Other dancers wear strings of shells around their ankles. The shells rattle when they move. Guerrero (ghe RARE oh) is an area near the Mexican coastline. Dancers from Guerrero wear white costumes. They twirl a white handkerchief when they dance.

Fajitas are often made on
Cinco de Mayo.

CHAPTER 8

Fiesta Food

SALSA

Salsa is a popular Mexican food. There are many varieties of salsa, but most are made from finely chopped tomatoes, onions, garlic, cilantro, and lime juice.

Mexican food is also an important part of celebrating Cinco de Mayo. Like traditional music and dance, Mexican food is different in each region. Favorites include tacos and burritos. These foods are made with tortillas (tore TEE yas). Tortillas are small, flat cakes that are made out of ground corn or wheat flour. Homemade tortillas are a special treat. It takes years of practice to learn how to make them. Corn kernels must be boiled and crushed to make the dough. The dough is patted by hand into round circles. The round circles are then baked in a hot pan. Most people

buy tortillas at the store. In the United States, they are often fried into chips or hard shells. But in Mexico, tortillas are soft like bread.

Flour tortillas are common in Northern Mexico. When the flour tortilla is folded around beans or meat and cheese it is called a burrito. Tri-Cities, Washington, is the home of the world's largest burrito. To celebrate Cinco de Mayo in 1999, people there made a 4,289-foot burrito. It weighed almost 4 tons. Over 6,000 tortillas were used to make it.

Cinco de Mayo is not an official holiday in the United States. Banks and schools are open, and post offices deliver mail. But it is the biggest Mexican celebration in the United States.

Ignacio Zaragoza, the general who led

Chalupas are another popular Cinco de Mayo food.

the Mexican troops at Puebla, was born in Texas. In Texas and other southwestern states, Cinco de Mayo is a day filled with activities. There are

Tamales are a spicy Mexican food that people enjoy on Cinco de Mayo.

parades, carnivals, and fireworks. Chili cook-offs and soccer games are held.

But Cinco de Mayo is a meaningful day for all Americans. After all, we too enjoy the peace and freedom that the heroes of the Battle of Puebla fought for. The Battle of Puebla proved to the world that North Americans could stand on their own. No outside force has tried to rule in North America since then. On Cinco de Mayo, we salute our friendship with our Mexican neighbors!

Cinco de Mayo Project

★

Mexican Flag

You can celebrate Cinco de Mayo by making a Mexican flag of your own to decorate with! You will need:

✔ **1 sheet red tissue paper**

✔ **1 sheet white tissue paper**

✔ **1 sheet green tissue paper**

✔ **1 sheet white construction paper**

✔ **white glue or rubber cement**

✔ **crayons or markers**

✔ **pencil**

*Safety Note: Be sure to ask for help from an adult, if needed, to complete this project.

1. Draw an outline of the Mexican flag on the white construction paper with a pencil. (A picture of the Mexican flag appears on page 24.)

2. Color the medallion in the center section of the flag with crayons or markers.

3. Tear the tissue paper into small sections, then twist each section. Make separate piles of red, green, and white.

4. Put glue or rubber cement down over each section of the flag except the medallion in the center.

5. Glue the twisted sections of tissue paper into place, leaving the ends sticking up.

6. When the glue dries, hang up.

Cinco de Mayo Project

Materials all ready!

Let's get to work!

Our Mexican flag is done and ready for Cinco de Mayo!

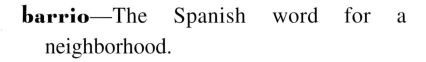

Words to Know

★

barrio—The Spanish word for a neighborhood.

bookbinder—A person who puts books together and attaches covers.

charro—The Spanish word for a Mexican cowboy.

corrido—The Spanish word for a kind of Mexican folk song that tells a story.

fiesta—The Spanish word for a party or celebration.

fort—A strong building for troops to stay in during war time.

mariachi—The Spanish word for a band with six to eight members that plays Mexican folk songs and other music.

Words to Know

★

revolution—A war that is meant to bring changes in the way a government works.

tortilla—The Spanish word for a flat, round cake that is made of crushed corn or wheat flour.

traje—The Spanish word for clothing or a costume.

Zapotec Indians—Natives of the Puebla region of Mexico.

zócalo—The Spanish word for town square.

Reading About

Harvey, Miles. *Look What Came From Mexico.* Madison, Wis.: Turtleback Books, 1998.

Johnston, Tony and F. John Sierra, illus. *My Mexico/México Mío.* Madison, Wis.: Turtleback Books, 1999.

Menard, Valerie. *The Latino Holiday Book: From Cinco de Mayo to Día de los Muertos—The Celebrations and Traditions of Hispanic-Americans.* New York: Marlowe & Company, 2000.

Palacios, Argentina and Howard Berelson. *Viva Mexico!: The Story of Benito Juarez and Cinco de Mayo.* Orlando, Fla.: Raintree/Steck Vaughn, 1996.

Riehecky, Janet. *Cinco de Mayo.* Danbury, Conn.: Children's Press, 1993.

Vasquez, Sarah. *Cinco de Mayo.* Madison, Wis.: Turtleback Books, 2000.

Internet Addresses

⭐

CINCO DE MAYO
<http://www.geocities.com/holidayzone/cinco/
index.html>

CINCO DE MAYO FOR KIDS AND TEACHERS
<http://www.kiddyhouse.com/Holidays/Cinco/>

CINCO DE MAYO PAGE
<http://www.hpl.lib.tx.us/youth/cinco_index.
html>

Index

★